In Light of Stars

Also by Bruce Willard

Holding Ground

Violent Blues

In Light of Stars

Bruce Willard

Four Way Books
Tribeca

What we don't touch, touches us.
Richard Jackson

Library of Congress Cataloging-in-Publication Data

Names: Willard, Bruce, author.
Title: In light of stars : poems / Bruce Willard.
Description: First edition. | New York : Four Way Books, [2021] |
Identifiers: LCCN 2021005300 | ISBN 9781945588945 (paperback)
Subjects: LCGFT: Poetry.
Classification: LCC PS3623.I5534 I5 2021 | DDC 811/.6--dc23
LC record available at https://lccn.loc.gov/2021005300

This book is manufactured in the United States of America and printed on
acid-free paper.

Four Way Books is a not-for-profit literary press. We are grateful for the assistance
we receive from individual donors, public arts agencies, and private foundations.

This publication is made possible with public funds from the
New York State Council on the Arts, a state agency.

We are a proud member of the Community of Literary Magazines and Presses.

Contents

iv.

Who was ever only themselves?
Forrest Gander

I start in the middle of a sentence
and move both directions at once.
John Coltrane

i.

FLIGHT SONG

After the business of dying was done.
After the last document was signed.

After the music of friends was risen
from church to a topless October sky

and decomposition
left just the colors of fall to burn

like small flags in the trees,
I learned to love what is incomplete:

the wood thrush working
on her song of flight tonight,

the moon chasing the sun
around the circle of sky.

Work indistinguishable from joy.
Water in a fountain cycling

as it seeks a way of being heard.
Because grace is nothing

when silence calls its name.

DRY

The sycamore leaves leathery,
flannelled one side,

a congregation of hands
across the lawn,

palms skyward,
waiting for rain.

The ground
is gunpowder;

anything
will set it off.

The Chinese say every storm
brings prosperity.

Six Septembers
our eyes have been dry,

red-lined, patient.
What becomes us

when the rains arrive?

AN IMAGE OF HEAVEN

One pattern in the sky means rain is close,
another, high winds aloft.

There's a way stars want to be seen
and contrails from the wings of planes in flight.

For the third straight day a mockingbird calls
from the rafter-tails of morning,

plying, questioning
the same circle of songs.

Time was, everything
had a pattern if I had time to find it.

Time was, a place
to sing, close

but not too close, to all I love.
Now I'm less sure

than of the opaque fullness
storm clouds withhold in summer

when we gather to hear the sound
of evening breaking apart:

audience for the rising clouds
of the afternoon,

fellowship with the lonely
starships of the night.

LISTENING IN THE BAMBOO

Twelve months since he left
and still I call
to hear his voice
message cadenced
and song-like,
the way at first light
I listen for warblers
in the bamboo, to know
everything's the same,
though nothing comes
the same way
when I am listening for it.

Every day the same music,
his bass barely audible
under whatever's leading:
the morning, the quiet playing
inside the bamboo's click
and bend, something featherless
as a flock of me dispersed
by what has passed

returning bird-by-bird
to the leaves—
a sound like brush-
cymballed cumulus,
brightly spaced

in a diminished sky
and the paling moon
which leaves me solo
with these birds.

FAMILY TREE

A man's clothes hang
in the tree beside his home.
Damp as confetti
the morning after an event.

They were not mine,
I swear,
though I knew the man
and watched him
climb the tree
like a friend
into the overhead light
of late mid-life,
unhanging, unchanging
each shirt, each suit.

The pants were longer
than the light
between branches.
They were not mine,
I swear,
though I knew the man.

I hid behind
the curtain
watching his small journeys
in and out of the home,

folded moments,
stains, I swear,
run red within
my purpled veins.

SOMETHING SAID

Not him wrapped in stripes.
Not the plans of him
removed from the body
before showing.
Not the song we sing.

What comes after.
Something said
years ago, his voice
traveling this far
through a windless sky.

INVERTED ROOT

i am going to make something
of this day

be still   concentrate
on the hands

each transition
each grace note

the sharp-less mode
the inverted root

there is much
rephrasing

each verse is a place
to spend the night

THE HALF-LIFE

Of his clothes
I kept one T-shirt.

Gray V-neck, Northern
Pacific patch in front.

The line ran out
years ago;

I don't know
if he ever traveled that way.

I liked its loose-necked
romance, its frayed sleeves,

summers with a splitting maul,
autumn put up in cords

of beech and sugar maple.
I liked the enduring stains

a life of silence
half-tries to vanquish.

The line by the house
doesn't go anywhere

you'd want to go.
There's a depot and side rail

one train crossing to the north.
A couple of boxcars gather wind

and wildflowers.
How do you decide

to move?
How do you decide

to do anything one last time?
The train never comes

and then it's gone: one echo fades
as the next comes into range.

What changes is the way
the sound moves one world.

I'm wearing the shirt today—
gray

with a little black
around the edges.

I can feel
its retired warmth—

old coal
between the rails,

once converting heat
to something like distance—

its half-life expired
as husks of clothing,

another crop of lupine,
or what remains
of a passing life.

ii.

COMING AND GOING

My grandfather was an engineer.
Collected tolls on bridges
at the Jersey shore.
A quarter for each crossing:
Longport to Seaview,
Ocean City to Strathmere.
My Scottish grandfather
who cussed all immigrants
and edged both sides
of his two-step lawn
with a long-handled roller-blade
where grass shouldered concrete.
Who kept the fence along the alley
painted and clear of poison.
My grandfather, who collected coins
each day and sat on the screen porch
summer evenings
with a can of Iron City
and a tin of Rold Gold
in the quiet company
of an immigrant wife
counting the days
as the world passed through.

MANY MOONS

Medals with his effects, a pocketknife
with one bolster, a tie clip like a locomotive.
Objects that celebrate, cut, and join.

A box of glass eyes he kept in a drawer—
four cloudy planets of deepening shades,
a different moon for every man.

The lightest held me as a child.
In the next I saw my first room,
the long shadows there.

The third eye sparkled,
sleight of glance and hand,
the measured strides

between one wall
and the next.
In the darkest eye

a reflection—
the space behind glass
where light holds fast.

POCKETKNIFE

It rode closed,
unopened,

close to the sensitive
parts of me

more than twenty
years. Passed

from my father
the promise

it could open
a letter or splice

a pair
of speakers:

those letters split
in time,

the copper
arteries bared

of insulation,
swollen with sound,

filling the quiet
rooms of our home.

MEDITATION

woodpeckers are flying
palm tree to feeder
to palm tree to birdbath
this morning the conga
of their brains feathered
with flight

scriptors of sky they coast
point to point
in loopy dips
calligraphy
circumnavigation
appetites willed

diet-weary of fall
they feast on sunflower
and raise their flaggy heads
in communion
water rippling
down their throats

as if hunger knew no pause
for breath
no road aches
for turns or hills

NOT QUIET

The sound of rain stopping.
The sound of the dog next door

when it quits barking
at the UPS truck on Hill Road.

The bent song silence makes
between the notes of a slow blues.

On my way from West to Main,
past the house with the pond

and the football that rests untouched
deep in the grass 9 months now

the thought of calling you
is not quiet

in an audible way
and it warbles

between the granite curbs
of each bridge I cross.

REVEAL

retreat of tires
on blacktop   each morning

stuttering of seamed
freeways   at night

I have travelled   recklessly
for a purpose

stars are syncopated
solos of light

you cannot hear them
when they are dark or close

we must try not to love too much
the rhythm that makes us

unforgettable   the road
which covers with turns

what it longs to reveal

STROKE

i.

To the teacher in third grade who asked what we wanted to be
Julie said, *Veterinarian* and I said, *Conductor*
and Billy made a *woo-woo* chugging sound.

A dumpster in the alley whinnied and crunched
and a mower on the playing fields across Maple
made a smoothing sound as if it were working to connect

the measures of a spring, New Jersey afternoon
to what would become a movement of anticipation.
Each triangle of sunlight and shadow

mixed in that high-ceilinged room
as if I were cardstock in a piece of SpinArt,
a card clothespinned to the fork of a bike,

a card in a deck of photos that could be thumbed
to tell a story, a motion picture of images moving
beyond the hands of their unscreening.

And it is still not enough.

ii.

I remember the fallout shelters on Nassau and Witherspoon.
And in the cleaving homes on Hodge, the canned goods,
fashionably shelved between leaded walls.

Books, supplies, games, beds ordered and made
as if it were possible to shelter abundance.
Wednesday afternoons we listened to the air-raid sirens

and moved to the basement of school, waiting for silence to bloom.
But it was not enough. The sounds of breathing, dogs,
traffic broke through. Each explosion of sound

filled the dim rooms: squeak of soles overhead,
whispers in diminished light. Not enough
to survive the shape of darkness.

iii.

There's a flutist in the paseo this morning, 3000 miles away.
His music gathers between shops and cafés. How his song collects!
Notes rising, glancing off walls, mixing with the sounds

of workers in kitchens, people at their plates triangulating the moment
into memory. The musician, one part of the history of everyone
playing that song, another moving inside its refrain.

iv.

I am close enough to break
the circle of my life, sitting on a bench in Radiology,
my ninety-one-year-old father next to me in an open-back smock,

waiting on a test for pneumonia. My hand circles
his freckled, bare shoulders and balding head and I'm reaching back
sixty years, touching him as he first touched me.

He tells how he's lived by the hands of men—boxers, gardeners,
billiard stringers, enlisted men, doctors, pianists, and accountants.
How he felt the hands offered to him,

surrounded himself with their touch. Warm, thin skin
sliding over bones. Knuckles in a satin sack.
His voice bent as the notes of a velvety blues.

v.

I am close enough to taste the powdered western dirt at my feet,
smell its flight as it whirls above sandstone and adobe, blows
in circles like the music I hoped to conduct.

There is no place,
no long words for what I hoped would be.
Not because the words don't exist,

or because they are not good enough.
But because there are new words
for the place that bodies meet.

Breath to gesture, stroke of skin on skin,
skin on string, wind on reed. Wind,
beautiful wind, in my face,
this morning, that becoming,
a bridge to be.

iii.

FEBRUARY, HIGH DESERT

Wide valley, ribbon road, miles
town from town. No radio

in this stretch, no cell to connect
to the bodies of other cells.

Low on fuel, vaporous
light of mid-February,

the sun earnest and longing.
A town with two street lights,

warm glow ponding
a wide street,

a service station with two bays,
double rack of retreads.

By one bay, restrooms;
in the back, a market.

Groceries, homewares,
circular card rack,

belts, hoses, wiper blades
on the wall. Beyond,

a lunch counter with six red vinyl
stools, young couple

minutes from their home
in white shirts, clean shoes,

two red envelopes on the table
between pepper and salt,

leaning into the late hour,
leaning into the night.

UNHINGED

At a gate in Salt Lake City airport,
I watched a hardware salesman,

his bag like a pilot's case, the kind with maps
of every airport he'd ever passed through.

His hands were full of receipts and papers,
between his legs a cup of coffee, no top.

How he strained
to still his knees,

keep the shaky liquid balanced
each time the connected seats were rocked.

His look of resignation when goodness
overflowed to his trousers,

darkening his crotch.
The sound he made

like a hinge on a door
that could not be closed.

RECEPTION

Did you make love to her
or her to you?

Was it the embrace
of her legs you sought?

A mouth can be
so misunderstood;

so many purposes
for the impression of lips.

A fullness
betrays the mind:

smile of acquiescence,
sneer of lust.

Put your hands together.
Which one

is touched?
Which one is touching?

There are many ways
of being received

but few ways
of knowing.

When I send a letter
I think of the opening.

When I receive one
I imagine how it was sealed.

AFTER ORAL SURGERY

When I wake I visit the islands of Chile
below Ushuaia, close but of another country,
disconnected from the mainland of my legs.
Regina and Kamloops, the permafrost prairie
towns of my jaw, are frozen
and everything south is calling:
the sandy elbows of Point Reyes
and Point Conception, the knuckles of Baja,
my Panama, Bogotá, and Machala.

Such distance traveled so early in the day
without removing my shoes or belt,
emotional support at my side,
earning miles before the birds of reason
have taken flight! How self-righteous
to recline and feel
no pangs of guilt. Death,
practically out of the question now,
a warm sack of fur next to me
like a natural reply, her breathing
ripe with the swell of morning—
ice plant, *frangipani*
and the smell of seaweed.

ART SHOW

We needed an alter
ego to bring us
together. A show
of unity for the multitudes
we contained. Something
to make us interesting
to ourselves.

The man in the beret
with *Fuck You* tattoos
 stood next to the woman
in Tory slides
 and an *I Love NY*
T-shirt. The bartender
 recycled Jewel-cups
of chablis and goldfish.

Some people wore
painted faces, others colored
hair, abstract
nails, sandals
like sculptures
climbing calves,
running shoes like sunsets.

And the paintings,
quiet at the perimeter,

waited patiently
for their turn
to say anything
unforgettable.

HISTORY LESSON

Ninety million years ago the sea was 600 feet higher
than it is tonight. No frost in the garden
to turn the avocados black and waxy,
to expose the thorns between each rose.
Sandy beaches stretched the length of Chile.
You could paddle to Greenland in three days.

But years of rain and heat
made choosing a vacation destination difficult.
A grief of storms accrued. And giant birds,
large as Lamborghinis, crossed continents of solitude
without a flap of their wings, riding the pre-nuclear
Vulcan winds months at a time,
confident the tides would change.

SONG SPARROW

That summer we opened the lake cottage,
prehistoric sound of loons before us,
decades of children at our back,
familiar sound of water
under the porch eaves.

A song sparrow
hit the window
just as summer began.

You held it in your hand
bent over, unable to breathe
another year, working
your fingers
under its feathers and bone.

THE RELEVANT

It doesn't matter
what it thinks;

you're analog,
fluid-filled,

a compass,
the kind by Silva—

red *Direction of Travel* arrow
on one end—

whose body,
a metaphor,

is known
by its referent.

It doesn't matter
where you're going.

You'll get there,
leg by leg,

one red eye closed—
standard deviation

your music—
dead reckoning

in your soul.

ABEYANCE

a voice on the corner
shouting in the face of night
liquor bickering with conscience
sleep with desire

a picket fence with a gate
you might step over
kitchen windows cranked
open to the street

below the smell of lilacs
entering like a ghost
searching for a single
hesitation to haunt

SONG

something cannot happen
without hands
i want to say
something cannot grow
without touch
can you hear me

somewhere is not
without hunger

 in the fields
in the kitchen
on a canvas
on a page
can you hear it

make a song
a trench
in the earth
sprinkled with
seeds

or a stave
like a perch

for the human voice
through which
arpeggios of sunlight
ascend

iv.

SANCTUARY

In a bathtub at the Sanctuary Motel,
water to my waist, listening
to the faucet exchange
warm for cold.

More drops than drips.
Drops like drums. Drums like dreams.
The syncopation takes me
back to a duplex, a kitchen
sink, my father bent over me,
white plastic tub
between his arms.

He sings, *Fly Me To The Moon.*
One hand steadies my shoulders
while the other orbits my chest with soap.
Each time the refrain comes 'round,
he croons: *In other words,*
hold my hand. His voice
is a ballad of vanilla and oak.

It's about the music,
I know. It's always
about the music.
But someone has to make it.
Someone has to push or pull,
stroke or touch.

My eyes can make day of night
or night of day.
I can index a second with smell,
make a tsunami with my hips.
I can re-call blue songs in my chest
that cause the tile walls to hum.

What do I make of the warmth
when the water has drained away?

DAUGHTER

It's Christmastime once more,
the end of the year,
and we're under the weather,
the season here but not quite
two weeks off,
asleep by nine
on the living room couch,

when she appears
at the base of the stairs,
handrail wrapped in ribbons,
lights rising up the bannisters,
leading us up
into the night,
suddenly holy
with stars.

FRUIT

So many years
not wanting
children

it was hard
to explain
the change.

Nothing
he could take
credit for.

It was the boy
who touched him
as flannel

touches evening,
the boy
who led him

toward what
he sought
to extinguish.

Then he was
all in,
deep and lost,

wanting to name
the shadows,
rewrite the story

as years later,
when his girls
offered their weight

to the morning,
he raised them,
right as oranges,

sweet and ripe,
longing to be carried,
drunk

until the goodness
was gone.

BETWEEN THEM

fish are boiling the mirrored water
of our cove this morning
a sound like small waves pushed ashore

two cormorants circle the bait ball
sending silver mackerel spinning
skyward toward the sun

I can see the teaming birds
work the dark salty water between them
the shadows of their longing

like you and I drawn to windows each day
or whatever light trips the vacancy
you perhaps with what you let in

to your box of rooms and mirrors
me with the names of words that got away

KAIROS

The morning after Thanksgiving
an offshore wind stands up waves
and calms the sea. Not a bird
on the feeder

this morning. A loose skirt
of bark uncovers
the eucalyptus's
leggy branches.

To give thanks is to expose
everything to nothing:
beat of memory, sound
of flying overhead.

In the salvia a blur
of invisible hunger;
motion before a
great and open window.

ALBATROSS

Great bird, who'd have thought
you'd fly so far? Soul on wings
motionless over the surface
that once swallowed you. Climbing,
diving toward ship's stern,
veering back again.

If all grief leads back to the world
what course takes you?
Aren't we all grounded
by the same calm?
Snow loads the slopes
of the Forbidden Plateau.
Ice binds the current of the Lemaire.

Time was a place
to cut out the hardness.
Chop at the frozen drift.

Listen. The ice is breaking.
One berg on another.
Glide, proud bird.
Stillness is making ground.

PEACE PIECE

Darwin was wrong about survival
but he knew about tears.
How lacrimal glands
are the aquifers of touch.

One day we may better know
the living language of water,
the sibilance of a stream as it loses
altitude and makes the longest word
known to humans and animals.

One day all species may be joined
by the consonance of waves
pulled shoreward
by our common need to be covered.

How many tears does it take
to fill a glass? A vase? A pool?
In the 19th century
women kept tear bottles
for men sent to sea or war.
Held the precipitation
of emotion in their hands
like a calendar, a reservoir
of love.

The brains of humans
shrink at night allowing streams
to pass through the muddy channels
of knowledge, washing away the day.
Aqueducts of data, hostility,
tributaries of indifference flushed
each night while we're sleeping,
recycled, carried
skyward and rained down
on a drought-bitten world.

Darwin was wrong about survival
but he knew how tears divine tears.
How we are joined
by what escapes us,
made whole by our undoing and loss.

BRIDGE

If you were here you wouldn't know the names
of the islands and outposts—British,
Chilean, Argentinian, and one Chinese,
Great Wall—that have survived
another polar winter. On the bridge
the words of our St. Petersburg crew
are in the tongue of a cold war
no one remembers. But they contain
the coordinates memory needs for reference—
Trinity, Deception, Cape Longing.

You'd remember the aging sound
of the engines, the way touch bridges
expanses of absence
and returns us to a place
we need to know, the familiar
instruments labelled in another language,
the twice-hourly bells
delivered in Russian
that timestamp our journey.

At these latitudes
the radar finds mostly ice.
It's impossible to fathom
what passes nameless

and unseen. Here, the wind
makes space of every surface.
Vanquishes air to air.

A name is reference
for the time it holds.
Watch me set yours
to the austral wind.

USEFUL ISLAND

64°43′ S 62°52′ W

It is night on the black water of Gerlache Strait.
Night in the souls of passing bergs.
Night in the breast of Albatross and Cape Kestrel,
and in the crevasses on Mt. Parry and Baldwin Peak.
It is night in the portholes of passing ships
and in the spirits of explorers.
Bold, kind, polar night.

And the night takes up
the gaunt shadows of evening
repatriating each absence
to the blackboard sky,
returning memory
as stars whose journeys
arrive like dust penned to slate,
awaiting more layers of dust.

And the sea archives its ice
as islands, pancaked on the surface,
broken by the blues of summer,
rejoined as clouds,
the color of new snow.

IN LIGHT OF STARS

If you sit without motion
starlight makes holes in the night
sky, liquid strained
so many years in silence,
the milky essence of childhood
streaks through.

What is there to say
of what binds us?
What passes through
the night without changing
burns out, wants someone
to burn with. Brother,

it's not for us to relive the bruises
the body becomes,
unseen, unknown.
I hope you have been drawn
someplace beautiful, held
by someone tight
in the creamy light of the moon.
There are so many stars
looking for a constellation
to join. Tonight,

let us partner the light,
imagine a line that connects
each astral point,
makes a story
we can tell ourselves
when it is dark
or beginning to rain.

Notes

"History Lesson" was inspired by a line in Jim Harrison's poem "Moon Suite" in *Dead Man's Float* (Port Townsend, Copper Canyon, 2018): "Birds are poems I haven't caught yet."

"Useful Island" refers to an island on the Argentinian side of the Gerlache Strait in Antarctica.

"Bridge" is for my father.

Acknowledgments

AGNI, Alaska Quarterly Review, Askew, Gunpowder Press' *While You Wait,*
The Harvard Review, Interliq, Maine Public Broadcasting Series, Miramar, Poet Lore,
Salt Journal, and *Spillway.*

Thank you to Laure-Anne Bosselaar, Chris Buckley, Kwame Dawes, Katie Ford,
Jeff Harrison, Major Jackson, Ahmad Jamal, Hale Milgrim, Joe Millar, and
Martha Rhodes for the reading, inspiration, suggestions, and support. Without
you, this could not have come together.

Thank you Jodie for your love and faith in images you did not speak in words.

Bruce Willard's poems have appeared in *5 A.M., AGNI, Alaska Quarterly, Cortland Review, Harvard Review,* NPR's *Writer's Almanac, Ploughshares, Poet Lore, Salamander,* and other publications. His first collection, *Holding Ground,* was published by Four Way Books in 2013. *Violent Blues,* his second book, was published by Four Way Books in 2016. Willard lives in Colorado and Maine. More information is available on the website www.brucewillard.com

Publication of this book was made possible by grants and donations. We are also grateful to those individuals who participated in our 2020 Build a Book Program. They are:

Anonymous (14), Robert Abrams, Nancy Allen, Maggie Anderson, Sally Ball, Matt Bell, Laurel Blossom, Adam Bohannon, Lee Briccetti, Therese Broderick, Jane Martha Brox, Christopher Bursk, Liam Callanan, Anthony Cappo, Carla & Steven Carlson, Paul & Brandy Carlson, Renee Carlson, Cyrus Cassells, Robin Rosen Chang, Jaye Chen, Edward W. Clark, Andrea Cohen, Ellen Cosgrove, Peter Coyote, Janet S. Crossen, Kim & David Daniels, Brian Komei Dempster, Matthew DeNichilo, Carl Dennis, Patrick Donnelly, Charles Douthat, Morgan Driscoll, Lynn Emanuel, Monica Ferrell, Elliot Figman, Laura Fjeld, Michael Foran, Jennifer Franklin, Sarah Freligh, Helen Fremont & Donna Thagard, Reginald Gibbons, Jean & Jay Glassman, Ginny Gordon, Lauri Grossman, Naomi Guttman & Jonathan Mead, Mark Halliday, Beth Harrison, Jeffrey Harrison, Page Hill Starzinger, Deming Holleran, Joan Houlihan, Thomas & Autumn Howard, Elizabeth Jackson, Christopher Johanson, Voki Kalfayan, Maeve Kinkead, David Lee, Jen Levitt, Howard Levy, Owen Lewis, Jennifer Litt, Sara London & Dean Albarelli, David Long, James Longenbach, Excelsior Love, Ralph & Mary Ann Lowen, Jacquelyn Malone, Donna Masini, Catherine McArthur, Nathan McClain, Richard McCormick, Victoria McCoy, Ellen McCulloch-Lovell, Judith McGrath, Debbie & Steve Modzelewski, Rajiv Mohabir, James T. F. Moore, Beth Morris, John Murillo & Nicole Sealey, Michael & Nancy Murphy, Maria Nazos, Kimberly Nunes, Bill O'Brien, Susan Okie & Walter Weiss, Rebecca Okrent, Sam Perkins, Megan Pinto, Kyle Potvin, Glen Pourciau, Kevin Prufer, Barbara Ras, Victoria Redel, Martha Rhodes, Paula Rhodes, Paula Ristuccia, George & Nancy Rosenfeld, M. L. Samios, Peter & Jill Schireson, Rob Schlegel, Roni & Richard Schotter, Jane Scovell, Andrew Seligsohn & Martina Anderson, James & Nancy Shalek, Soraya Shalforoosh, Peggy Shinner, Dara-Lyn Shrager, Joan Silber, Emily Sinclair, James Snyder & Krista Fragos, Alice St. Claire-Long, Megan Staffel, Bonnie Stetson, Yerra Sugarman, Dorothy Tapper Goldman, Marjorie & Lew Tesser, Earl Teteak, Parker & Phyllis Towle, Pauline Uchmanowicz, Rosalynde Vas Dias, Connie Voisine, Valerie Wallace, Doris Warriner, Ellen Doré Watson, Martha Webster & Robert Fuentes, Calvin Wei, Bill Wenthe, Allison Benis White, Michelle Whittaker, and Ira Zapin.